sacred sex

embracing your sexuality
as God designed it

tony evans

MOODY PUBLISHERS

CHICAGO

Editor: Christopher Reese
Interior Design: Ragont Design
Cover Design: John Hamilton Design, LLC / Erik M. Peterson
Cover Photo of watercolor copyright © 2012 by Petek ARICI/iStockPhoto.
All rights reserved.

Library of Congress Cataloging-in-Publication Data

Evans, Tony, 1949-
   Sacred sex / Tony Evans.
     p. cm.
   Includes bibliographical references (p.   ).
   ISBN 978-0-8024-1155-6
   1. Sex--Religious aspects—Christianity. I. Title.
BT708.E935 2012
241'.664—dc23

                              2012004947

We hope you enjoy this book from Moody Publishers. Our goal is to provide high-quality, thought-provoking books and products that connect truth to your real needs and challenges. For more information on other books and products written and produced from a biblical perspective, go to www.moodypublishers.com or write to:

Moody Publishers
820 N. LaSalle Boulevard
Chicago, IL 60610

3 5 7 9 10 8 6 4 2

CONTENTS

SEX AS GOD INTENDED IT

The December air greeted us with a chilly embrace as we made our way out of the house, down the hill in the backyard, and across the field. Having grown up in urban Baltimore where concrete was far more prevalent than trees, I had definitely stepped into a foreign environment.

Lois and I were in the middle of enjoying a Christmas getaway with some close friends who lived in a rural area. But on this Christmas, we got much more than the normal holiday brunch and shared conversations. On this trip, I got a lesson in skeet shooting as well.

Now, anyone who knows me knows that skeet shooting and Tony Evans aren't exactly best friends. In fact, prior to this event, I can't recall ever even picking up a gun. I'm a sports man. As the chaplain for both the NBA

Mavericks and the NFL Cowboys, I get to regularly witness competitive sports that involve hand-to-hand contact—or at least body to body from time to time. As a former football player myself, I like my recreational activities to include sweat, guts, and sheer force.

The idea of holding a gun, pulling a trigger, and watching a clay target possibly break apart into pieces didn't do much for me. But as the polite and grateful guest that I am, I went along for the supposed adventure. Anyhow, who doesn't love a challenge? Certainly I could knock those clay birds out of the sky like the best of them.

Wrong.

The first clay bird flew. I aimed. Shot. Got nothing.

Then the next one flew, and I aimed again. Still nothing.

And again. Nothing.

Again. Nothing.

Now, even though the years may have matured me, my vision is still 20/20. And my hands are still steady. I had seen the object in the air. I had aimed. I had pulled the trigger. Yet the clay birds just kept flying.

After a few too many flew away and my friend no doubt saw the perplexity come over my face, he walked over to me and said, "Tony." Placing his hand on my shoulder, he proceeded to explain both the art and science of skeet shooting. "Tony," he said my name again. I think he wanted me to make sure and listen closely. "The clay object is like a bird. When it's released, it is flying across the sky just like a bird. It's moving. So if you want to shoot it out of the sky, you can't aim at it. If you aim at it, by the time your pellets get there, it will be long gone. In order to shoot the skeet out of the sky, you have to get in front of it. You have to be ahead of it. Your aim must always go before it."

I took my friend's advice and decided to apply it. He made sense. So I regrouped and called out, "Pull."

Up flew the clay bird.

This time I squeezed the trigger while aiming out in front of it.

BAM!

That bird was destroyed! Obliterated. Toast. Pieces of it rained down from the sky.

Now you may be wondering whether this is a book on skeet shooting or sacred sex. Or what could skeet shooting have to do with sex at all. But if you picked up this book looking for a heart-to-heart on God's view on sexual purity, you've done the right thing. Because that's exactly what it's about.

> **WHAT WE VIEW AFFECTS WHAT WE DO. GUARD YOUR EYES AND YOU WILL GUARD YOUR ACTIONS.**

But before we begin looking into the sacredness of sex, I want you to realize the power and pull of sex itself. No other activity consumes us as humans more than sexuality —for good or for bad. And, sadly, it is mostly for bad. Sex is a strong force—a force as we will see that is often driven by physiological and chemical reactions that have the potential to place it in a position of dictating to you what you will do rather than you dictating to it what you will do.

How you handle yourself, or fail to handle yourself sexually will have everything to do with where you aim. You must get out in front of it. If you think that it is something you can decide on in the heat of the moment, that bird will fly. If you think that you can make up your mind where that so-called "invisible line" is that you won't cross when you reach it, that bird will fly. If you choose to dabble here or dabble there in sexually explicit television shows, music, movies, or even porn—that bird is going to fly. A recent study showed that teens who watched a high level of programming with sexual content were twice as likely to get pregnant over the next three years as those who didn't.[1] What we view affects what we do. Guard your eyes and you will guard your actions.

The only way to successfully handle the power and force of this dynamism called sex is to go out before it. You must draw your boundaries ahead of having to use them. You must choose to outwit it and out aim it. You must understand it, take charge over it. And, most importantly, always be in front of it.

YADA AND YOU

One of the most revealing principles I ever discovered about sexuality from the Bible took place when I was preparing to preach a few years back on an entirely different subject. In the middle of studying for and getting ready to dive into a twelve-week sermon series on the subject of knowing God, I came across a powerful reality about sex.

In fact, so powerful was this truth that it became the backdrop in the series for illustrating the depth of the relationship that God desires to have with each one of us. Because as we all know, sexual intimacy involves far more than merely two bodies experiencing contact and exchanging fluids. If that were all that was required for intimacy to occur, then prostitutes would be the most intimate people in the world.

But in the Hebrew language, we discover something incredibly powerful about sexuality. When we uncover the intent of the original language, we learn that sex is designed to involve plumbing the depths of another being in such a way as to both *know* and *be known*—much more than mere physical contact, and only attainable in an atmosphere of total and deserved trust.

Anytime you study Scripture and you want to discover either the meaning of a term, phrase, doctrine, or principle you come across, it is always best to approach it according to the hermeneutical *Law of First Mention*. This is important for a number of reasons, but primarily because the concept of origination is significant in Scripture.

For example, the Bible itself begins with the phrase of origin, "In the beginning." Then it proceeds in the book of Genesis to lay out and address the origins of not just the creation of the heavens and the earth but of every foundational theme throughout the remainder of Scripture: sin, worship, covenants, redemption, and even the type, or foreshadowing, of the Savior to come.

The *Law of First Mention* states that the original meaning or definition of what is being studied is to remain constant throughout one's study unless the text itself tells you to change it at a later point.

Again, what does hermeneutics, skeet shooting, and Genesis have to do with sex? Everything. Because in order to get out in front of your own sexuality where you are dictating to it rather than it dictating to you, you need to understand God's viewpoint and intention in creating it.

So in accordance with the Law of First Mention, we see that the very first time Scripture mentions sexual intimacy is in Genesis 4:1, where we read, "Now the man *had relations* with his wife Eve, and she conceived and gave birth."

The Hebrew term used in the very first account of sexual intimacy for "had relations" is the word *yada*.[2] It is the same word used a few verses earlier when describing that Adam and Eve's eyes had been opened and they "knew" that they were naked. It is also the same word used when we read, "Then the Lord God said, 'Behold, the man has become like one of Us, *knowing* good and evil'" (Genesis 3:22).

The word *yada* is not a word referring to body parts or physical activity. In all definitions of the word *yada*, which occurs over one thousand times in the Old Testament, it means:

- to know, learn to know
- to be made known, be revealed
- to make oneself known
- to cause to know
- to reveal oneself
- to know by experience

Each time *yada* is used in connection with relational interaction, it indicates plumbing the depths of the reality of another person—or even plumbing the depths of the reality of God Himself. In fact, it has the capacity to be so intimate a term when applied to relational involvement that God uses it to refer to His own relationship with us when referencing the absolute closest of interactions:

The secret of the Lord is for those who fear Him, and He will make them *know* (*yada*) His covenant. (Psalm 25:14)

"You are My witnesses," declares the Lord, "And My servant whom I have chosen, so that you may *know* (*yada*) and believe Me." (Isaiah 43:10)

I will give you the treasures of darkness and hidden wealth of secret places, so that you may *know* (*yada*) that it is I, the Lord, the God of Israel, who calls you by your name. (Isaiah 45:3)

In each of these descriptions, God speaks of His relationship in a close and intimate manner. We read about "treasures of darkness," being "chosen," and God's self-obligatory relationship He establishes called "His covenant." On top of that, twice we read the specific word "secret"— once in reference to God's secrets, "the secret of the Lord," and also in relation to what God will give—"hidden wealth of secret places."

One thing that is always true about secrets is that you have to be pretty close in order to share them. Of course you have to be close intimately by way of trust, but oftentimes that also includes being close in proximity.

When you were younger and you wanted to tell someone a secret, what would you normally do? If you were like me, you would get next to the other person close enough so that you could lean over and with your hand cupped around your mouth, you would whisper in his or her ear.

That is the typical way of sharing a secret.

And that is what God says He will do with those who know (*yada*) Him. He will be so close that you can hear Him whispering in your ear, telling you the secrets that are reserved for those who have a special relationship of intimacy with Him.

Yet what is essential to realize is that when God chose to *yada* us, He chose to do so with a people who are perishing (John 3:16), have gone astray (Luke 19:10), and are condemned (John 3:18). God gave the perfection of His *yada* to those who knew only imperfection (Romans

3:23). He revealed the purity of Himself to those who are desperately wicked (Jeremiah 17:9). And He was able to do all of this while maintaining His holiness, because Jesus hung on a cross as a sacrifice for the sins of us all. Jesus not only died, but He died to Himself as we read, "He humbled Himself by becoming obedient to the point of death, even death on a cross" (Philippians 2:8).

Likewise, the very foundation of true *yada* of one another in the security of the marriage union is rooted in a sacrificial dying to yourself in such a way that means laying your will, pride, and needs on the altar while considering the other as more important than yourself. It is in this sacrifice where both partners die to themselves that what is new can grow and flourish in the soil of biblical love.

This is because in sacred sex the two partners share much more than some moments of passion. They share their secrets, their fears, their hopes, their failures, and even so much as their "treasures of darkness and hidden wealth of secret places." They reveal themselves in a way unlike with any other. And within that revelation, if it is truly *yada*, they will find the most authentic form of love possible.

In fact, the secret nature of what they share becomes its own treasure.

Because how do you make a secret no longer a secret? You tell it to others.

It is the same thing with the sacredness of sex. Sex is no longer able to be a sacred shared experience—it is no longer *yada*—when it is no longer unique between the two who share it. If and when sexual relations become something common—something shared by those other than the ones bound by a *yada* relationship, it changes from being what God had originally intended into that which Satan corrupted it into—known in Scripture as *porneuō*[3] or *shakab*.[4]

Both of these terms refer to the same physical activity as in *yada*, yet both remove the sacred and replace it with the common—thus removing one of the main purposes and intentions of sexuality, the exclusive unveiling of knowing and being known.

And when this is done, as we see repeatedly through Scripture, it brings with it heartbreak, jealousy, regret, and severe emotional, physical, and even spiritual consequences. For example, we do not read *yada* in reference to the following, but rather *shakab*:

- David and Bathsheba
- Tamar's rape by Amnon
- Lot's daughters' sexual activity with him
- Shechem defiling Dinah
- Reuban and his father's concubine
- Even Jacob and the wife he did not choose, Leah

A person can engage in physical relations with another person and not experience *yada*—not share the intimate and sacred realities of the depths of who they are. That is merely sex, and not sacred sex. Yet this is not what God intended when He originally created the sacred act of sex. This is not how God chose to introduce the concept of sexuality to us in its origin in the garden.

The primary principle to remember and hold on to in guarding your sexual purity and keeping sex sacred is God's original intention for sex—a shared, unveiled revealing involving knowing and being known.

Keep in mind, the very nature of a veil is predicated on keeping something hidden or secret. If not, it becomes a scarf or a head wrap, not a veil. Likewise, *yada* can quickly deteriorate into *shakab* or *porneuō*—carrying with it the inevitable outcomes associated with sex in the absence of a sacredly shared trust.

> SACRED SEX INCLUDES MORE THAN JUST THE BODY—IT INCLUDES THE DEEPEST PARTS OF THE SOUL AND THE SPIRIT AS WELL.

COVENANT BOND

Sacred sex includes more than just the body—it includes the deepest parts of the soul and the spirit as well. It includes the covenant. This is because the deepest purpose for sex is to inaugurate, or initiate, a covenant. In order to fully comprehend the sacredness surrounding sex, we need to look at it from our Creator's perspective rather than our culture's perspective. It would be easy to think today with the sexual emphasis in our music, movies, and magazines that sex was born in Hollywood rather than birthed in heaven.

But sex was never designed to simply be a mechanism for biological fulfillment. It was not simply designed to address the problem of raging testosterone or elevated hormones. Sex was designed to both inaugurate a covenant and to renew it.

The closest thing in the Bible to sex, as a corollary to the covenant, is baptism and communion. Baptism is the initial public act you take before witnesses to validate your desire to be wedded to Jesus Christ in covenant. And communion is the ongoing action you take that, as often as you do it, renews this commitment to the covenant.

Consummation of a marriage on the wedding night is designed to inaugurate a covenant. And basically, from that point on, as often as you do it, you renew the covenant and commitment that was inaugurated on the wedding night.

In Scripture, covenants were frequently established by blood. For example, God made a covenant with Abraham, the sign of which was circumcision (Genesis 17:10–12). All of the males born in Israel were to come as young boys and have the foreskin of their sexual organ removed to signify that they were part of God's covenant people. In this way, they were to be unlike everybody else.

Why was circumcision chosen as the sign of the Abrahamic covenant, which would establish Israel as God's special people and through which Abraham would become the father of many nations? Because this covenant was fulfilled and expanded as Abraham and his male descendants produced children.

Therefore, their sexual organs would bear the mark of the covenant as a special sign that they and the children they fathered were set apart to the Lord. The rite of circumcision involved blood, which was part of the covenant.

So it is in marriage. Look at Deuteronomy 22:13–15:

> If any man takes a wife and goes in to her and then turns against her, and charges her with shameful deeds and publicly defames her, and says, "I took this woman, but when I came near her, I did not find her a virgin," then the girl's father and her mother shall take and bring out the evidence of the girl's virginity to the elders of the city at the gate.

The evidence was the bloodstained sheet or whatever garment was on the bed on which the couple consummated their marriage on the wedding night. Read the following verses and you'll see that if the parents could prove their daughter's virginity, she was acquitted and the husband was fined.

But if there was no blood, meaning the woman was not a virgin prior to her marriage, she could be put to death (Deuteronomy 22:21), because the covenant of marriage was inaugurated by blood. God created a shield around a woman's sex organ, which is called a hymen, that was to cover her until her wedding night when it would be broken and blood would then be shed over the male sex organ. This was designed to consummate a covenant as an unbreakable bond between two people and God.

CHEMICAL BOND

While a covenant is a spiritual bond between two people and God, the act of sexual intimacy also creates a physiological bond between two people. Sex doesn't necessarily take place in the bedroom. Rather, advances in scientific research have revealed that sex takes place between the ears—in the chemical connections occurring in the limbic portion of the brain.

On a practical level, this involves the diencephalon (which contains both the thalamus and hypothalamus parts of the brain.) The acts of viewing, hearing, smelling, seeing, cuddling, arousal, and orgasm involve a highly complex mixture of chemicals, each designed to regulate an intended response by our Creator.

Within the boundaries of a marital relationship, these chemicals serve the greater purposes of maintaining commitment, either heightening or lessening territorial responses of a male, fostering an environment for procreation and protection, and encouraging the transition from lovers to parents and back to lovers again, as needed.

Yet outside of the boundaries of a marital relationship, the chemical bonds that are created and then broken when partners change leave lasting scars, cravings, holes, and even symptoms of withdrawal. While science may have only recently come forward with an explanation for why and how sexual relationships create such strong bonds physiologically—and therefore leave such excruciating pain when not cemented in the context of a secure marriage—God's Word has told us this same truth all along.

When Paul wrote to the citizens of Corinth at the height of moral and spiritual decay in that society, his word choice accurately reflected what happens when sex occurs. He said,

> Or do you not know that the one who *joins* himself to a prostitute is one body with her? (1 Corinthians 6:16)

What is most interesting is Paul's use of the word "join." The original Greek language uses the word *kollaō*[5]. *Kollaō* literally means, "to glue together, cement." Under the inspiration of the Holy Spirit, Paul's letter to the Corinthians was as scientifically sound as any of the articles or studies in the most recent medical and psychological journals of our day.

Sexual activity, and its subsequent release of brain-changing chemicals, literally *glues* or *cements* people together. When it comes time for those two people to part ways, a painful physiological reality occurs—primarily among women whose limbic system, which houses these chemical stores and grooves, is generally larger than males.

What is often worse is that unlike in the cases of drug addiction, cigarette smoking, porn, or even alcohol—we rarely validate the extreme physiological suffering that a woman, and even men, suffer as a result of illicit sexual relationships gone awry. And because this pain is not addressed, repentance is not called for, and healing is not encouraged. These same women and men often end up right back in the same place they once were, trying again to fill the emptiness or craving with someone new.

This is because a strong physiological reaction occurs in the brain that is very similar to reactions that occur with drugs, alcohol, and other addictive behaviors. And to stop the behavior without going through the steps of forgiveness, healing, empowerment, and freedom from it, will often only lead that person right back to what he or she had tried to stop. It would be similar to taking away the favorite brand of beer from an alcoholic and then sending him back into a bar with countless other brands to choose from. Would he have stopped drinking his favorite brand of beer? Yes. But would he have the emotional, physical, and spiritual tools necessary to turn down the opportunity to try another brand on another day? Probably not.

That is why it is important for you as a Christian to not only understand the *spiritual* reasons for maintaining a lifestyle that guards the sacredness of sex, but that you also understand the *physiological* reactions and interactions you are dealing with if you have engaged in illicit sex in any form, even if it did not include going as far as intercourse.

Because unless you understand what you are seeking to deal with physiologically in overcoming sexual strongholds or temptations in your life, you will be aiming at the clay bird rather than out in front of it. And, as a result, you will miss your target every time.

Before we move on, I want you to be aware of a few of the powerful chemicals and their effects that are involved in sexual activity:

> **THE PROBLEMS ARISE WHEN A CHEMICAL CONNECTION IS MADE OUTSIDE OF A SPIRITUAL COMMITMENT.**

Oxytocin. Oxytocin has gained the reputation of being the "cuddling hormone" because it cements a connection between the two people involved. Studies have shown that oxytocin contributes to attachment and increases trust, and can even be released, once the attachment has formed, by something as simple as looking at a photo of the other person, hearing his or her voice, or intentionally thinking of them.[6] While the cementing of this connection promotes a healthy and stronger marriage, it also creates a glue—or tie—among two people who are not married if they engage in sexual activity—even sexual activity that does not lead to orgasm. This creates emotional and psychological tears when the source of the oxytocin is no longer there or another source has been called on to substitute. This can frequently contribute to depression, an inability to function sexually, and anxiety.

Dopamine. Dopamine is often referred to as the "rewards neurotransmitter." Dopamine is frequently associated with addictive behavior such as smoking, chemical addictions, or even risk-taking recreational activity such as high-impact sports or skydiving. It has a chemical structure similar to morphine. Within the process of sexual activity, dopamine supplies feelings of enjoyment, connection, euphoria, and calm that produce activity in the "reward system" of our brains. Because all forms of sexual activity have the potential to increase levels of dopamine, they can become addictive, whether through the physical act of sex, pornography, fondling, or masturbation. Each of these serve to connect the brain's reward system to the activity or person that produced the reward.

Adrenaline. Adrenaline increases the circulatory system while dilating the arteries to increase blood flow. Increased adrenaline can come through sexual activity or even through recreational activities such as bungee jumping. People in search of an "adrenaline rush" often need more in the activity later on to provide the same rush the next time. When coupled with contentment in a monogamous marital relationship, adrenaline is an ongoing benefit to an already enjoyable experience, keeping the intimacy alive over a lifetime. However, when the desire for adrenaline is not maintained in a stable environment, it can produce a lack of contentment in the existing relationship, resentment over dissatisfaction, and an addiction to seeking more of it through other, possibly illegitimate means.

A number of additional chemicals such as serotonin, testosterone, and estrogen were created by God in connection with the act of sexuality, parenting, and maintaining long-term relationships. The problems arise when a chemical connection is made outside of a spiritual commitment. The chemicals in and of themselves are not bad—in fact, they are good and bring great pleasure to a marital relationship based on the principles of sacred sex.

But when the chemicals are connected to the fluctuating ups and downs of broken relationships, they can produce great pain and deep psychological wounds. It would be similar to getting addicted to heroine and then stopping it cold turkey. The desire, attachment, and craving would remain due to the chemical impression made on the brain. If the decision to stop heroine stayed in place, in order to satiate the craving and numb the pain, another addictive chemical producer would be sought. And a cycle of addictive behaviors, or symptoms related to pulling away from addictive behaviors (such as depression, confusion, irritability) would occur.

In essence, heroine will have made a lasting impression, or groove, in the brain that doesn't go away simply because the substance is no longer around.

A similar thing happens with the chemical processes involved in sex. Pile up enough pain from the cementing and tearing apart from different partners, and you end up with countless people either turning to sex again to try to alleviate the pain or fill the emptiness, or to other forms of coping such as spending, alcohol, overworking, drugs, and other addictive behaviors.

Keep in mind that oxytocin has been known to be produced through something as simple as engaged eye contact, subtle touching, and hugs. None of these are bad when managed properly. Oxytocin is a positive chemical God gave us to bring happiness and solidify connection in our lives and relationships. It is only when high levels of oxytocin are created through an illegitimate attachment with someone who has not entered into a covenantal relationship of marriage with you that it becomes damaging in the long run. Especially when that relationship either ends or dissipates over time.

Once that chemical is present and does its work on the brain—particularly a woman's brain since women tend to have a larger deep limbic system than men—it is difficult to forget it, dismiss it, or satisfy it legitimately outside of marriage.

God's teaching on the sacredness of sex and keeping the sexual relationship pure between two married people joined by covenantal commitment is nothing to take lightly. Knowing how deeply addictive, gluing, and cementing the sexual relationship is, God gives us His warning clearly: "Flee immorality. Every other sin that a man commits is outside the body, but the immoral man sins against his own body" (1 Corinthians 6:18). He or she also sins against their own brain, along with their body, in light of all the potential damage that can be done physically and spiritually.

When sex is kept sacred—when it is a *yada* relationship between two covenanted parties in marriage—it opens up the pathway toward true intimacy and knowing.

But when sex is casually misused, it creates cemented bonds that when broken leave the lingering symptoms of insecurity, pain, abandonment, disrespect for self and others, and increased neediness for another attachment. This causes suffering in the present and also reduces the ability to establish proper boundaries in future relationships.

Paul's warning to the Corinthians to not join (*kollaō*) themselves with another in an immoral relationship is a warning to everyone today as well. In order to protect the sacred act of sex, you must aim for the standard God has given us in His Word. You must aim for *yada*.

2

THE VALUE
OF SEXUAL PURITY

A number of years ago I took Lois to play tennis. I will never do that again. After explaining the game to her, I showed her where to stand and told her that I was going to hit the ball onto her side of the net.

When I threw the ball up and hit it over the net the very first time, I knew I was in trouble. Instead of moving to the ball and hitting it back to me, Lois stood there with one hand on her hip, holding the racket as if to say, "You don't expect me to chase that ball, do you?"

I knew this was going to be a long day.

So I hit the ball over the net again, and once again, Lois watched it. I tried to explain to her that in order to play tennis, she needed to run after the ball and then hit it. But she replied, "Tony, I am not going to get sweaty out here running after a little ball. If you want me to hit the ball back to you, you need to hit the ball right to me."

Needless to say, the next time I hit the ball right to her. Yet instead of hitting it back to me, she took a Hank Aaron swing at it and sent it soaring over the fence. With her hand back on her hip, her look said, "Aren't you going to go get it?"

Instead of going to get it, I said, "Lois, let's go home. We can't play tennis outside of the rules."

If you want to enjoy the game of tennis, or any sport for that matter, you can't play by your own rules. You can't run only when you feel like running. That is not how you play. That is chaos. In order to play the game, you have to play within the boundaries set up that govern it.

UNRESTRICTED SEX IS BEING TOUTED AS A SHORTCUT TO PERSONAL FULFILLMENT AND SATISFACTION.

My humorous time with Lois on the tennis court that day actually illustrates a very serious truth that we are looking at in our time together: You can't enjoy sex the way God intended you to enjoy it if you refuse to stay within the lines or boundaries He has made.

But the fact is, our culture is standing there like Lois, hand on hip, and saying, "I don't want to play by those rules. I want to play my way." If you want to know our culture's values and attitudes on sex, love, and moral purity, just listen to its music.

I grew up with popular singing groups such as the Temptations, the Miracles, the Impressions, and the Dells. I still occasionally turn on these groups while I'm driving in my car or listening to music at home. The basic message of their songs was "I love you. You love me. I lost you. You lost me. Can we get together again? Maybe." Not bad, and it came with a beat.

Yet today, the music seeking to shape our young people's moral attitudes goes by titles like "Sex on My Money" and "Sexy Back."

Sex dominates our popular culture to a degree we've never seen before. Prime-time television and the movie industry would be lost if they couldn't exploit sex. Talk shows wouldn't have anything to talk about without sex.

Unrestricted sex is being touted as a shortcut to personal fulfillment and satisfaction. People have given up their virtue for sex, traded their families for it—and now they're getting sick and dying because of it.

While sex is a wonderful and beautiful gift of God designed for human fulfillment, Satan has taken this God-ordained activity and has done with it what he does best. He has counterfeited it and sold his cheap imitation as the real thing.

So men lose their virginity trying to validate their manhood. Women sacrifice their purity seeking for someone to love and accept them. We have bought Satan's lie that immediate sexual gratification, regardless of the long-term cost, ought to be the driving force in our lives.

But the price tag for this purchase is high indeed: high in medical costs for AIDS and sexually transmitted diseases. The physical consequences of sexual immorality may last a lifetime or cut a lifetime short.

It is also high in the shame that sends people to professional counselors. It is high in the death rate as unwanted children are aborted on the altar of convenience. It is high in welfare costs as the government doles out money to take care of children who don't have a pair of parents to watch over them. And it is high in the divorce rate. Clearly, the misuse of sex under the direction of Satan is decimating our society.

Sex is God's idea, and, therefore, it is good. But like anything else that God makes, when people get their hands on it and redefine it according to their own agenda, what is good becomes destructive. What was created in heaven becomes a mixture from hell.

That is what has occurred in the area of human sexuality. There is no place you can go in Western civilization to run from it. All you have to do is get in your car and drive down the highway—the billboards will let you know that sex sells. Some people will tell you that this blatant openness about sex is good because Christianity has suppressed and denied sex for too long.

I beg to differ. God has no hesitancy in talking about sex. He does not run from it. He does not blush when He deals with it. His Word puts it on the line when it comes to telling the truth about sex, which is what I want to do as well in our time together.

Abandoning God's Standard

To say that God puts a very high value on sexual purity is to understate it. The reason people give sex away so easily is that they don't know how valuable sexual purity is in God's eyes. Stuff that you think is cheap, you throw away. Stuff that you think is expensive, you hold on to.

When God created Adam and Eve as opposite yet complementary sexual beings with a natural attraction for each other, Adam's statements about Eve in Genesis 2:23 show he understood that they were created for each other. And when God joined that first pair in marriage, there was no hesitation and no shame in their union. Theirs was the first and only perfect marriage, because sin had not yet polluted everything.

When God creates something, it produces ecstasy and not shame. With Adam and Eve there was no "I should not have been there. I should not have thought that. I should not have done that." Whenever God does something, people are going to feel good about it. They don't have to hide.

Obviously Adam and Eve were virgins before their marriage, so they had no reason to feel shame. It's true they were also sinless at this point, but the entrance of sin did not change God's sexual standards. Men and women were still expected to be virgins before marriage.

There were no double standards such as we have today, where men in particular make excuses for their sin by saying things like, "Well, I'm a man, and you know how men are about sex." No. You don't set the standard; God does.

I'm really concerned about this because we are raising a generation of young men, and even boys, who are like the dog I used to own. When my dog wanted to satisfy his sexual desires, he went looking for a female dog. His standards weren't very high. All he was concerned about was that his partner was a female.

When he came back home, my dog showed no particular concern about what he had done. He ate and slept as if nothing happened. Whether that female dog was now carrying his puppies was of no concern to him. All he knew is that his passion had been satisfied.

What we have today is what I call the "Alpo crowd," a generation of men whose sexual standards are no higher than my dog's. They could not care less about the consequences to the woman. And they are not about to take responsibility for any children they may father. So our society picks up the tab for their irresponsibility as we pay for the consequences in our culture.

That is what happens when people abandon God's ideal for sex. Culture suffers under the weight of a generation of unwanted and uncared for children, women with no one to marry, and men who have badly misunderstood the meaning of masculinity.

Another tragedy today is that if your kids are in public school, they are most likely going to get some harmful and wrong information. Even if your school does not dispense condoms, the "safe sex" mentality still overshadows a lot of what is taught.

Yet God says something entirely different. God's sexual standard outside of marriage is virginity, an extremely valuable gift from Him that you can give away only once and never get back again. Yes, there is forgiveness for sin, and a person who has fallen sexually can rededicate himself or herself to Christ. But immorality in any form does tremendous damage. We must fight for a return to God's standard.

A BIBLICAL VIEW OF SEX

The church at Corinth had sexual problems. The Corinthians lived in a sex-obsessed city, a port city where ships docked from all over. Corinth was the New York or the Los Angeles of its day. It was the place to be—built to service all of this activity and all of the merchants and sailors who came around.

In fact, on a hill in Corinth sat the temple of Aphrodite, the goddess of love. This temple was divided into two halves. On one side was a restaurant and on the other side was a brothel. People would go to the restaurant for dinner and then visit the brothel. Essentially, the brothel was made up of rooms that housed a thousand or more "sacred" prostitutes who engaged in sex with worshipers as part of their pagan rites.

> SEX IS PART OF YOUR GOD-GIVEN DNA, BUT IT WAS NEVER DESIGNED TO BE YOUR MASTER.

Because of this, Paul had to explain that having sex is not the same as having dinner. The people in Corinth were misguided about sex because their attitude was that sex was like food. When you get hungry, you eat. When your body craves sex, you do the same thing with your sexual drive that you do with your hunger. You satisfy it.

But Paul had a word for them, and it is a word for us as well. But before addressing the difference between food and sex, though, Paul made a very important point about sexual passion in general when he said, "All things are lawful for me, but not all things are profitable. All things are lawful for me, but I will not be mastered by anything" (1 Corinthians 6:12).

What he was saying was that God has rules that govern how we use what we have been given.

Sex is a legitimate and lawful passion given to us by God. So if you are struggling sexually, you don't pray that God will take away your sexual passion. You are then asking not to be human. What you pray is that you not be mastered by your legitimate and lawful sexual passion so that the expression of it becomes your obsession no matter what God's rules say. Sex is part of your God-given

DNA, but it was never designed to be your master.

You see, freedom does not mean doing whatever you *want* to do. Freedom is doing what you *ought* to do. Suppose a man stands on top of a tall building and says, "I want to be free from gravity. I am going to do my own thing. So let me serve notice on you, gravity. I am in charge now. I am free." He jumps off the building, and for a couple seconds he is free. But it doesn't take long for it to dawn on him that he is not as free as he thought. That is confirmed as they sweep him up off the pavement. Gravity was in charge all along.

The sidelines in football are designed to contain the game. Suppose the halfback decides, "I don't feel like being tackled today. I don't like sidelines. I think I'll run up into the stands, out into the concession area, into the parking lot, come around to the other side, run back through the concession area, down the stands, back onto the field, and across the other team's goal line for a touchdown. After all, I'm free." That's not freedom. You can't have football without sidelines. You cannot enjoy sex the way God designed for sex to be enjoyed if you operate outside of His rules either.

Sex is like a fire. Contained in the fireplace, a fire keeps everybody warm. Set the fire free, though, and the whole house burns. You don't want the fire in your house to be free. You want it contained so that it can generate warmth and not destruction.

And while sex is like a fire, it is not like food—a major distinction that Paul needed to draw for the Corinthians, as

I mentioned earlier. Paul made this distinction in the very next verse where he said, "Food is for the stomach, and the stomach is for food, but God will do away with both of them. Yet the body is not for immorality, but for the Lord; and the Lord is for the body" (1 Corinthians 6:13).

The Corinthians were right about the food part in that the stomach was created for food. In other words, when you get hungry it is okay to eat because God has designed a compartment to receive the food. There's no great issue involved, because someday both food and your stomach will be obsolete. But sex cannot be equated with food—there is much more at stake. God did not put us on earth so that we could indulge our sexual passions. We are to use our bodies—that is, our lives—to glorify Him.

But someone might say, "Everybody else is doing it." God's answer is, "Since when are you everybody else? Since when does the crowd dictate what you are supposed to do?"

Many Christians today struggle with sexual sin like the Corinthians. We are all susceptible to it. It all stems from the same root—our sinful flesh, nurtured by a secular worldview that causes us believers to be governed by what the culture says and not by who we are in Christ. We all face it.

So the question is not whether we have a sexual appetite. The question is, What legitimate avenue has God given us through which to satisfy that appetite? By way of a reminder, God's only legitimate avenue for sexual expression between two people is marriage. Unless you start with this foundation, you are going to believe and act on the lie that you are free to have sex whenever you feel like it. You are going to buy into the line that "this is just the way God made me."

Another difference between food and sex is that what you eat does not affect what happens in eternity, but sex does. In fact, your morality affects your inheritance in eternity. We read, "Neither the sexually immoral . . . nor adulterers nor men who have sex with men . . . will inherit the kingdom of God" (1 Corinthians 6:9, 10 NIV). Paul states clearly in this passage that your sexual immorality will affect your inheritance in the kingdom of God. It will also affect what you receive when you stand before Christ and He offers you your reward (1 Corinthians 3:12–15).

In 1 Corinthians 6:14, Paul continues his eternal perspective when he talks about God's resurrection power. He writes, "Now God has not only raised the Lord, but will also raise us up through His power." Remember, he's talking about the body here. What part of us will be raised from the dead someday? Not our spirits, which never die, but our bodies. What Paul is showing is that our bodies have significance beyond the grave, so what we do with our bodies has eternal consequences.

The question that must be answered is this: Do we really believe that God's power is so great that He will transform our dead bodies someday and raise us into eternity, yet His power is not great enough to help us control our sexual passions today? Anyone who believes that does not understand the resurrection power of Jesus Christ. You do not have to be owned by your passions.

The resurrection of Christ is proof that we have power to control the passions of our bodies until such time as God provides an outlet for them in marriage.

We looked at this passage earlier in the first chapter, but it bears repeating here where we read the next verse Paul writes in 1 Corinthians 6:

> Do you not know that your bodies are members of Christ? Shall I then take away the members of Christ and make them members of a prostitute? May it never be! Or do you not know that the one who joins himself to a prostitute is one body with her? For He says, "The two shall become one flesh." But the one who joins himself to the Lord is one spirit with Him.

The believers in Corinth were part of a pagan Greek world that taught a two-tiered view of the universe. The Greeks believed that the spiritual and the physical were on two completely separate levels. Therefore you could do what you wanted with your body and not affect your spirit.

God says no to that view. The body and the spirit are closely linked. For the Christian, sex is a spiritual issue. You cannot worship God on Sunday and enter into sexual immorality on Monday and keep those separate, because your body, and not just your spirit, is for the Lord. In fact, as a Christian, anytime you engage in sexual activities whether it be physically or even mentally, Christ is right there with you.

Like a woman who takes drugs while pregnant, thus making her baby an involuntary participant in her drug habit, when you engage in sexual immorality as a child of the King, you make Jesus an involuntary participant in what you are doing.

As a Christian, you have been bought with a very high price—the death and blood of Jesus Christ. You are no longer yours. You are owned by Christ, "For you have been bought with a price: therefore glorify God in your body" (1 Corinthians 6:20).

Your body is now the temple of the Holy Spirit, which means that every time you have sex or engage in sexual activities physically or mentally, you go to church.

The temple was a place of worship so, fundamentally, wherever you are and whatever you are doing, you're having a worship service. Ask yourself the next time you think about engaging in immoral sex, whether that is something you would do in the sanctuary. Because that is what you are doing. Your body is the sanctuary of the Holy Spirit.

Likewise, in these verses, Paul tells us there is no biblical view of sex without commitment. The only lawful use of sex is within marriage, where two become one. You don't have sex in order to have commitment. You make a commitment first, and then celebrate it with sex. You don't say, "Let's try it, and then I will see whether I want to marry you."

No. You marry me, and then you try it. Women, don't

get played by smooth-talking men who want to show you love without committing to the love they want to show you. Why? Because you are more valuable than that. You are too valuable to be a party favor of immature men who only want to gratify their libidos.

Instead, hold your head up high and declare your value. Ask him, "Are you willing to put your life on the line for me?" Buying you dinner and a movie is not a commitment. But when you enter a lifetime commitment, that is when you are to express your sexuality together.

Paul is not saying that sex outside of marriage is wrong simply because two warm bodies come together. Something much more significant is happening. Sex outside of marriage is the ultimate lie because two people are performing the act of marriage without the covenant. No such thing was ever intended in God's economy.

Many people, even believers, who have been married for a long time are still suffering from the scars of things that took place perhaps in their teenage years. The reason is that there is no other sin quite like sexual sin, because every other sin is external in its effect. But immorality does damage to the soul.

Why? Because, as we have seen, Paul says that when you engage in physical intimacy, that engagement produces a new thing. The two people become one. There is no other realm, other than when you are joined to Christ in salvation, where this kind of intimacy happens. Not only that, but as we saw earlier, there are chemical imprints being made in your brain that solidify the connection of sex. It is like taking sodium and matching it with chloride. You wind up with table salt, which is something brand new. In the same way, when you mix two parts hydrogen with one part oxygen, you get water. When you bring two people together through the sexual relationship, Scripture says that you wind up with something brand new.

Now if you decide that you don't want the new thing you just created, if it was just a momentary passion or a fling, then you break it apart. But in the breaking apart, you tear away a piece of yourself. Obviously, the more times you do this, the more withdrawal you experience and the greater the loss that you feel.

Anyone who has kids knows what it's like to try to get chewing gum out of the carpet, especially after someone has stepped on it. It's a challenging experience trying to pull that gum out without leaving any behind. The merger of the gum with the fiber in the carpet has so integrated them that to get out all the gum, you have to tear away some of the carpet too. And you usually leave some of the gum behind anyway.

So it is when there is a merger of two people in sexual intercourse. When they try to tear that relationship apart, they tear themselves, and a part of them is left behind as well.

GUARDING YOUR SEXUAL PURITY

You say, "Tony, this is tough. I want to maintain my purity, but sex is all around me. What do I do?" Paul has a two-word answer for you in 1 Corinthians 6:18: "Flee immorality." In other words, run! Get out of there. Move your feet. Aim ahead of the temptation. Be out in front of it with boundaries and coping techniques.

You can't emotionalize, theorize, or play with sexual temptation. You have to hit the track and get out of there. You cannot keep placing yourself in environments that are sexually tempting to you and expect to stay clean. That may mean changing your viewing and reading habits, your dating habits, or even your friends.

One of the most successful singles in history was a very handsome, smart young man probably in his mid-thirties and committed to God. His name was Joseph. Look at Genesis 39:5: "It came about that from the time [Potiphar] made him overseer in his house and over all that he owned, the Lord blessed the Egyptian's house on account of Joseph; thus the Lord's blessing was upon all that he owned, in the house and in the field."

Let me tell you something about Joseph. He was from a dysfunctional family. His brothers were murderers, thieves, adulterers, and connivers who sold Joseph into slavery. His father, Jacob, was a polygamist. Joseph was from a troubled family, but he turned out fine. As we will see, he held to his purity at all costs.

Does this mean you can have a messed-up family and still turn out fine? Yes, it does. Does this mean you can recover from abuse and live a pure life before God? Yes, it does. You may not have had any control over what happened to you, but part of dealing with it today is understanding that if God is in your life, He can help you make a fresh start.

Verse 6 tells us that "Joseph was handsome in form and appearance." Someone might say that if Joseph is this clean sexually, he has got to be a nerd. No, he was good-looking. He caught women's eyes. He was well built. The brother had it going on.

Besides this, Joseph now had some money in his pocket because he had a good job. And he had power because he was over all the house of Potiphar, an important Egyptian official. He was everything any man would want to be.

But Joseph never let the external control the internal. He never let how other people viewed him control what he knew about himself. Joseph belonged to God. He was God's man, and, as a result, he was able to handle what happened next in verses 7–9:

> It came about after these events that his master's wife looked with desire at Joseph, and she said, "Lie (*shakab*) with me." But he refused and said to his master's wife, "Behold, with me here, my master does not concern himself with anything in the house, and he has put all that he owns in my charge. There is no one greater in this house than I, and he has withheld nothing from me except you, because you are his wife. How then could I do this great evil and sin against God?"

This is powerful stuff. Joseph did not let somebody else's passions control his decisions. Now, this was one needy woman. I take it that Potiphar was always gone because he left everything in Joseph's care. Joseph was always there. Perhaps she was saying, "I'm being neglected, and I have a problem." But Joseph was saying, "I'm not your solution."

What a beautiful contrast to men who prey on women they know are vulnerable. They find women who may be single, who they know are alone and feeling lonely, and who are probably struggling with sexual temptation, and these men present themselves as the answer to a woman's emotional needs through sexuality.

Joseph did not let Potiphar's wife control his actions because his body belonged to God. Notice the focus of Joseph's concern at the end of verse 9. Sexual sin, like all sin, is ultimately against God. Joseph had never read 1 Corinthians 6, but he knew the principle that his body was not his own.

Now I wish I could tell you that once you take this kind of stand, the temptation will go away. We know better than that from Joseph's story. Mrs. Potiphar kept after him "day after day" (Genesis 39:10).

You probably know what happened. She grabbed him one day and said, "Lie with me!" (Genesis 39:12). What did he do? He fled. He left his garment and hit the road. Joseph lost his shirt over this deal. He left his shirt in her hand and fled the house.

Now, please notice. Joseph did not say "Let me counsel you" or "Let's talk about it." He got out of there. He ran. It cost him dearly to take a stand, because the woman accused him of rape, Potiphar believed her, and Joseph wound up in jail (Genesis 39:20).

Listen to me: if you decide to guard your sexual purity at all costs, you are going to pay a cost. If you are a man, when some people find out you are taking your stand, they are going to put you down and punk you out. They are going to question your manhood. If you are a

> # THE ACT OF SEX MEANS THAT A SPIRITUAL RELATIONSHIP HAS TAKEN PLACE.

woman, some people will think you're uptight. Your friends may accuse you of being too scared to have fun. Some men may try to test your commitment.

If you commit yourself to sexual purity, you may feel as if you're all alone in a mental prison like Joseph was in a literal prison. There is a cost to pay, but with God, there is also a payday. Read on in Genesis, and you'll see how God honored and blessed Joseph by elevating him to a high government position in Egypt. God gave him a wife and two sons—and even brought his brothers back and changed them so that they repented.

It may cost you to be faithful to God, but when God rewards you, it will be worth the cost.

THE DESTRUCTIVE NATURE OF IMMORALITY

Go back to 1 Corinthians 6 and look at the rest of verse 18 again: "Every other sin that a man commits is outside the body, but the immoral man sins against his own body." There it is. When you develop a lifestyle of immorality, it is unlike any other sin in its destructive nature.

Drugs can't compare to sex in its destructiveness. Crime can't compare with it. Nothing can compare with it because sexual sin carries its own built-in, self-deteriorating mechanism. Why? Because of what we said above: Sex uniquely combines the physical and the spiritual.

The act of sex means that a spiritual relationship has taken place. So when it is an illegitimate spiritual relationship and you back out of it, you back out with spiritual as well as physical and emotional damage. Many people don't even know that this is what they are battling in their marriages—the holdover from things that happened earlier but have never been dealt with.

The immoral person is like a man who robs a bank and gets what he wants for the moment, but then has to pay the price for a lifetime once he is caught. However, the morally pure person is like a depositor in the bank who puts his money away where it is securely held as the interest builds up, so that he can really enjoy it when it is time to draw on his account.

What we are seeing in our world today is the destruction being wrought by men and women who have taken God's idea of sex and contaminated it. God places a great deal of value on virginity and sexual purity in marriage.

Friend, since this is not the message your culture is giving you, you in particular are going to have to be counter-culture. You are going to have to go against the crowd, which as I have suggested may mean being laughed at and called things you don't want to be called because you hold to a standard that most of your peers don't buy. But you're not alone, because that's true for all of us who belong to Christ.

Paul did not skip the subject of sexual morality because he couldn't. He lived in a decrepit world full of incest, debauchery, and prostitution. His world was morally contaminated, and here were these Christians at Corinth, and I'm sure in other places, who had all kinds of questions: How do I control myself in a world like this? What should my attitude toward marriage be?

Sounds familiar, doesn't it? What we're facing is nothing new. Divorce was common in the New Testament world. In fact, in Paul's day it was not uncommon for someone to have been married twenty times. A man could get rid of his wife for almost any reason—she couldn't cook, she was getting a little overweight, the wrinkles were starting to come—wrinkles the husband had no doubt caused. Nevertheless, all these ridiculous things became grounds for divorce.

Paul stepped into this madness to tell Christians they had to go against the culture. As we saw earlier, he argued that God created sexuality and therefore He must define it. Any definition of sexuality that leaves God out is a defective definition of the term—and a destructive one.

So the immoral person sins against his own body. That is, when we engage in immorality, we start to self-destruct. There is no area of life that can bring such internal damage, Paul says, as this one.

Paul has a word for single people and for married couples as he transitions in chapter 7 of his first letter to the Corinthians in answering the questions they had written to him. He gets right to the heart of the matter in verse 1: "It is good for a man not to touch a woman." That word *touch* means to light a fire, which was understood as a euphemism for sexual passion and activity. Paul says that it is good if that fire is not lit because, once it's lit, it is very hard to extinguish. And, once it's lit, that fire can easily burn out of control.

Since Paul says that it is good not to light the fire of sexual passion, the Bible's word to singles is that your singleness can never be good unless it is celibate. And to those who are married, your marriage bed is only as good as it is pure. You are not to light anyone else's fire, so to speak.

If you are single and acting as if you are married—that is, if you are unmarried but are physically involved with another person so that you are functioning as married people—that is not good. Your singleness will never be good under God until it is a celibate singleness. If you are trying to live in two worlds at one time, you will never know the good and God-honoring single life Paul talks about. In fact, Paul speaks so favorably of singleness that he says, "I wish that all men were [unmarried] even as I myself am" (1 Corinthians 7:7).

Singles, if you really want to maximize your singleness, you should avoid lighting the fire of sexual passion in order to abstain from immorality. Then God will bless and use your singleness, and you will find the fulfillment and meaning and direction He wants you to have.

So Paul says that to avoid immorality, what men and women must do is save themselves for marriage. The fact is that some people were so sexually active before they got married that they were running on low octane after they got married. Their passions burned too early, and now they had burned low because they did not keep what was special and sacred for the marriage bed. This helps to explain the high sales of Viagra and other performance-enhancing drugs.

Young woman, don't let any player tell you that because he washed his car, got his hair cut, got all shined up, took you out, and spent all this money on you, that he's done his job and now it's time for you to be the party favor. Tell him to forget it. He can't make sexual advances on you just because he did any of those things. He can take his money and go home. Tell him good-bye.

Why? Because you are not for sale. Remember, after the intimacy, when he walks away, he takes part of you with him and leaves part of him imprinted on you. Outside of marriage, you have no sexual obligation just because a guy is nice. Until he is willing to give all of himself to you, he can demand nothing from you. If he says, "If you loved me, you would," you say, "Because I love you and because I love me, I won't."

God's idea is that the sexual relationship is to be preserved for one man and one woman in the context of marriage. Sex is not a way to say thank-you for a nice evening. Sex was not given for you to release tension or explore a hobby. Sex was not given just so that you can feel good. It was given to express your total commitment to another person.

So you wait until God gives you that person. You pray for that person. Then, when God grants you that person, you express your commitment in the intimacy of that relationship to the max.

It is a very serious thing to unleash one's sexuality outside the safety of a lifelong, one-flesh marriage. Marriage is God's only method for safe sex.

3

Keeping
Sex Sacred

Paul was not a prudish, self-righteous single person who looked down on those who could not control their passions. It is possible that Paul was married at one time, because he might have been a member of the Sanhedrin, the Jewish ruling council, whose members were required to be married.

Whether Paul was called to be single, a widower, or whatever, we don't know. We do know that he speaks forthrightly about the subject of the intimacy of marriage and does not apologize for it.

Look at verse 3 of 1 Corinthians 7: "The husband must fulfill his duty to his wife, and likewise also the wife to her husband." This word *duty* can cause great concern. Is marital intimacy supposed to be a duty? What does Paul mean? He is talking about physical intimacy being designed to be other-focused—this is what my mate needs.

Now, I am not saying that every single unbeliever in every single case is self-motivated. And I would not try to claim that every Christian marriage reflects the ideal of selfless giving. I'm talking about what ought to be an overall pattern.

By the way, Paul's order in verse 3 is important. It's the husband's responsibility to take the lead, and his wife's calling is to respond.

Many men have said to me, "I would love to fulfill my duty to my wife, but she won't let me." That could be because what you are offering to fulfill, she does not need. One of the great challenges in building true physical intimacy is understanding what the other person needs.

What a woman needs starts in the morning and not at night. What a woman needs starts in the kitchen and not in the bedroom. What a woman needs starts with her emotions and not with her body. When some husbands say they want to meet their wives' needs, they are talking about something far different from what their wives understand by that phrase.

If a husband is really serious about meeting his wife's needs, he will talk with her more, he will compliment her more. He will still be dating her and showing her love when he has nothing else on his mind but an expression of affection. Listen to me if you are a husband—if the only time your wife knows she has your undivided attention is at 10:00 p.m., when you want to get it on, if she knows that the only time you are going to compliment, recognize, esteem, and value her is then, because you have not met her emotional needs, which began at 10:00 a.m., you are not fulfilling your duty to your wife.

> **When needs are met in marriage, physical intimacy is a natural outcome.**

That is why 1 Peter 3:7 tells us husbands to understand our wives. Most of our wives were attracted to us at least in part because of what we did during the dating period. One thing we were able to do was talk in a way that caused her to respond positively.

Another thing a lot of men were good at when they were dating their future wives was making them feel special, and planning little surprises. They would open the car door and wait until she got in, then close it softly behind her. Now she is lucky to get in before he drives off. When she was about to go through a door, the guy would open it for her. Now the door hits her as he walks through ahead of her.

See, husband, what made your wife want to marry you was not your stripping off your clothes and talking about your physical attributes. It was the fact that you met many of her needs. When those needs are met in marriage, physical intimacy is a natural outcome. In other words, a husband is not fulfilling his duty to his wife unless he is providing what she needs.

This will be a shocking revelation to many husbands, but I'll risk it anyway: one of the best ways to find out what your wife needs is to ask. To assume that what you are offering is what the other person needs is the height of foolishness. Wives tell us they need affection and a sense of security, communication, and a sense of being cared for and esteemed.

That is why, when the romance leaves a marriage, the wife's passion for sex often dies. Not so with men. Men aren't as concerned with all of that relationship stuff. It's nice, but it is extra. You can make a man mad at 10:00 p.m., and at 10:05 he is fine and ready for some fire. You make a woman mad at 10:00 a.m., and, if that thing is not fixed, she is not fine at 10:00 p.m. In fact, she may not be fine at 10:00 p.m. for a month.

I'm not saying it's good that men are like this. I'm saying that's the way it is. We men have a long way to go in learning the art of intimacy with our wives. We need to learn that for our wives sexual intimacy involves the whole person and the whole house. It involves the compliment you make about the meal, how you come in the door when you come home from work, and how you treat her when she comes home from work, if that's the case.

When couples come in to see me and say they have a sexual problem, that is rarely true. In most cases what they have is an intimacy problem, a relational problem. Because of this, they cannot get the physical part of their marriage working. But the physical is not the problem.

The fundamental issue is expressed in that word *duty*. Husband, your duty is to your wife, not to yourself. When many men say "I want to meet her needs," what they really mean is "I want her to meet my needs." That is not what Paul says. He says that the issue for the husband is his wife's needs. Until a husband is willing to take the time and make the investment in order to understand his wife and her needs, he will never be able to meet them.

Now, Paul knows this is a two-way street. The second half of 1 Corinthians 7:3 is as important as the first half. If a husband is meeting his wife's needs, her duty is to reciprocate, to respond.

In other words, wife, your husband cannot date you and care for you and compliment you and serve you, and make sure your needs are met, only to have you deny his needs. You cannot be on the receiving end and not on the giving end. You cannot receive his love and affection and not meet your duty to him.

Look at verse 4: "The wife does not have authority over her own body, but the husband does; and likewise also the husband does not have authority over his own body, but the wife does." When a husband is fulfilling his duty to his wife, the wife responds and meets her responsibility to her husband by coming under his authority or lead.

The wife relinquishes the lead of her body to the touch, the care, the caress, and the love of her husband. Then, as the husband responds to his wife's response, he also relinquishes his body to her. The picture here is of two people who are learning that they belong totally to each other. In some mysterious way, when two people are intimate there is a giving of themselves, a vulnerability, and a mutual yielding.

See, to most of us, sexual purity means we're going to talk about premarital sex and how to keep yourself pure until marriage and avoid temptation and all of those issues. But the Bible's picture of sexual purity takes in the whole range of our sexuality, including marriage. What we are talking about here is as important a part of the subject of sex as all the premarital and extramarital issues.

If you have read the Bible much, you know that the Song of Solomon contains the Bible's most unblushing description of sexual intimacy in marriage. Chapter 4 describes the buildup to intimacy in great detail, and the beauty of it is that you see the self-giving between Solomon and his wife, the mutual yielding of their bodies. Notice that the intimacy begins with Solomon's compliments and words of admiration and appreciation for his bride, not with the physical act of sex. But when the moment of intimacy occurs, God Himself invites the lovers to enjoy one another (Song of Solomon 5:1).

When this kind of intimacy occurs within marriage, God blesses it. When it occurs outside of marriage, God condemns it. God so believes in this kind of marital intimacy that He recorded it, detail for detail, in the Bible.

When I delivered this message, I asked the men in my church some practical questions. When was the last time you dated your wife? When was the last time you surprised her? When was the last time you caressed her in a nonsexual way, or noticed the new dress or the new hairstyle? When was the last time you picked up the phone and simply said, "I just called to say hello. I am in a hurry, but I just can't get my mind off of you"?

See, husband, when you meet your wife's needs, she then responds by welcoming you, by letting you know that she is willing to give up her body to you. There is nothing that can match this kind of intimacy. This is how God intended it.

COVENANT SEXUALITY

Keeping sex sacred is something that all of us at one level or another have to come to grips with. It's a constant challenge to keep it in proper perspective. I say *all of us* because the sacredness of sex goes much deeper than the physical. We see this when we take a look at the seventh commandment, "You shall not commit adultery" (Exodus 20:14), in light of Christ's revelation on that command. We read His words, "You have heard that it was said, 'You shall not commit adultery.' But I tell you that anyone who looks at a woman lustfully has already committed adultery with her in his heart" (Matthew 5:27, 28 NIV).

The seventh commandment that Jesus referenced followed the sixth commandment, which was "You shall not murder." Killing is the death of a life. Adultery is the death of a relationship. What makes the two parallel is that both commandments have the death penalty connected with them (Exodus 21:12 and Deuteronomy 22:22–24). With such a penalty, the immoral act of adultery was evidently a serious infraction.

Carried forward into the New Testament, God states clearly that those who go outside of the boundaries of sacred sex (by fornication—unmarried illicit sex, and adultery—sex where one or both parties is married to someone else) will be judged. We read in the book of Hebrews, "the marriage bed is to be undefiled; for fornicators and adulterers God will judge" (Hebrews 13:4).

> WHILE THE LAW FOCUSED ON THE ACTION, JESUS FOCUSED ON THE HEART.

This is because adultery is defiling the bond of the covenant. And what Jesus has told us is that this covenant is defiled even when a man looks at a woman with lust—not to mention when two people engage in immoral sex. Jesus lets us know that adultery is deeper than the physical act because it is rooted in a spiritual source.

While the law focused on the action, Jesus focused on the heart. In stores today you will regularly see signs that tell you that in order to prevent shoplifting, they have hung surveillance cameras throughout the store. This is in order to reveal the hidden attempts at stealing what is not yours. Jesus says that God has a surveillance camera on your heart and that anyone who looks at another person with lust has already committed adultery. Even if it's only meditating on a single image or multiple images of another person or people in your mind through fantasizing, you are stealing something that is not yours.

When a man looks at a woman with an intentional look—and I don't mean the passing glance to observe beauty because God created women beautiful and admiring beauty is not a sin—but when a man elongates the glance, or takes it further in his mind, that is lust.

Pornography is immorality—whether it be hard porn in magazines or soft porn in the movies or music videos. Playing vulnerable women is immoral, whether it ends up in the bedroom or in your mind. As Peter writes, "With eyes full of adultery, they never stop sinning; they seduce the unstable" (2 Peter 2:14 NIV). These are the men who look for the woman's face that reveals she is either sad, neglected, going through emotional turmoil, or needy, thus knowing that her "unstableness" creates an opportunity for her to be easily seduced. The men who do this are men "with eyes full of adultery."

Women, be cautious of any man who presents himself as your rescuer, savior, or deliverer from your pain, emptiness, or the neglect you may be experiencing. These men may be looking to take advantage of your vulnerability. They may not be around once the thrill of the conquest has been satiated.

Take, for example, Amnon, King David's son, who made it his goal to lure his half-sister Tamar into bed with him. After he eventually set her up through manipulating the situation, she still did not consent to have sex with him. So he raped her (2 Samuel 13). Everything changed, though, after Amnon had gotten his way with Tamar, and his once feverish love turned into an intense hatred. We read that Amnon, "hated her with a very great hatred; for the hatred with which he hated her was greater than the love with which he had loved her. And Amnon said to her, 'Get up, go away!'" (2 Samuel 13:15).

Be careful of a man who will not take no for an answer. Even though he may talk more smoothly than anyone else you have ever heard, ladies, and even though he may shower you with his love—that love can quickly turn to disdain when the physical gets out of control.

Paul tells us in his letter to the church at Thessalonica that God does not take lightly this matter of sexual immorality, and in particular the matter of defrauding someone else in the matter. In fact, he tells us that God "is the avenger" in this when he writes,

> For this is the will of God, your sanctification; that is, that you abstain from sexual immorality; that each of you know how to possess his own vessel in sanctification and honor, not in lustful passion, like the Gentiles who do not know God; and that no man transgress and defraud his brother in the matter because the Lord is the avenger in all these things, just as we also told you before and solemnly warned you. For God has not called us for the purpose of impurity, but in sanctification. (1 Thessalonians 4:3–7)

He says do not defraud your brother in this matter. Obviously, to defraud is to steal. If you're married, He says, don't steal from your brother what is not rightfully yours. If you're single, then you're still stealing because you're stealing from the brother who is to be. All of us who have gone to college have heard the talk of the guys who wanted to party with the loose women, but wanted to marry the virgins. In other words, they wanted to defraud, but they didn't want to be defrauded.

But there is a lot of defrauding going on in our culture today because so many people are turning to sex to try to solve their problems, inflate their egos, or salve their pain. Yet turning to illicit sex simply exacerbates the existing problems rather than solving them because that is not what sex was designed to do.

Imagine if you were stranded out on an ocean and surrounded only by saltwater. Even if you were dying of thirst, you shouldn't drink the saltwater. Now, I know what you are saying, "But I need the water. I'm stuck out here."

You do need water; it's just that saltwater is not the water you need. You see, when you drink saltwater, you take in so much salt that your kidneys are unable to sift it through your system. So all that does is make your kidneys want more water. But the only water you have has salt in it. Eventually your kidneys shut down and stop working while the very thing you drank to try to save your life ends up taking your life. You die of thirst in a sea of water because the saltwater was never designed to satiate your thirst.

It is amazing the number of people who seek to solve their problems by using sex illegitimately. And, yes, an eight-second orgasm can give you a momentary release, but your problems remain. God's Word is clear that sex outside of marriage will only create problems rather than solve them. In fact, as we saw earlier, God Himself is going to be one of those problems created because He "will judge" and is "the avenger."

RECLAIMING YOUR PURITY

As we wrap up our time together, I know that many of you reading these pages may be wondering what happens if you have already lost your purity. Or what if you have already gone outside the boundaries of the sacred nature of marital sex. If this is you, I have good news for you because Scripture is full of people just like you who struggled in this area of sexuality, experienced the consequences of it, repented, and were made whole.

It doesn't matter how much you have done, or even how mis-used you have been. God offers forgiveness and cleansing if you will seek Him for it. A dirty diamond is still a diamond. It just needs to be cleaned.

Every week, I take my dirty clothes to the cleaners. When I drop them off, they are smelly, wrinkled, and worn. Yet when I go and pick them up the next day, my clothes are clean again, pressed, and smell fresh. This is because they have gone through the process of removing the dirt that was on them.

Jesus has a cleaning service. At Jesus' cleaning service, He picks up dirty people who have allowed, for one reason or another, their lives to take a turn down the wrong path. And at His cleaning service, Jesus knows just what to

> **REMORSE SHOULD NEVER BE CONFUSED WITH REPENTANCE.**

do to wash you and make you clean again. But you need to go to Him and ask Him to do just that. If you are involved in an illicit sexual relationship, using porn, or dabbling in any kind of sexual immorality, you must stop it, repent, and begin the process of seeking forgiveness, offering forgiveness, and being healed.

Simply stopping it is not enough. If you are dealing with unconfessed moral sins, then that is why you have no peace. That is why you have no power, no sense of God's presence, and your prayers are not being answered. Because when you don't come clean with God, He doesn't hang out with you. Yet renewing your intimate walk with God involves more than just stopping the sin you are committing or choosing not to commit it again. It even involves more than confession. In order to experience power and His presence in your life—after you confess your sins to Him—it is essential to pursue and nurture a close and intimate relationship with Him. It is in the abiding with Christ that you will discover true peace.

While pleasure has the potential of producing in you

a momentary satisfaction, it can never lead to peace. Only true repentance can begin the process of restoring intimacy with God and producing peace within your spirit. But keep in mind that there is a monumental difference between simple remorse and true repentance. In fact, remorse is what is often felt in connection with sexual immorality, especially when consequences have arisen. But remorse should never be confused with repentance.

Remorse leads to death while repentance leads to life. Consider both Judas and Peter. Both committed sins of betrayal against Jesus. Both felt bad about what they had done. In fact, we read that Judas "felt remorse" (Matthew 27:3). Judas's remorse was so strong that it even led to confession. The problem was, though, that Judas's confession didn't appear to be directed to God, but rather directed to men. We read that he returned the thirty pieces of silver and told the elders, "I have sinned by betraying innocent blood" (Matthew 27:4).

The next verse tells us that Judas then went out and hanged himself. His remorse did not lead to pursuing a restored relationship with Jesus or healing. It led to death. However, when Peter experienced remorse over denying Jesus, we read that "he went out and wept bitterly" (Matthew 26:75). So far we don't see any tangible difference between Judas's remorse and Peter's sorrow. However, the critical thing to remember about repentance is that repentance includes more than sorrow. Repentance includes a change of mind that results in a change of actions. It means both to turn from what you are doing *and* to turn to what is good.

It is evident that Peter had repented because when Peter later heard that Jesus wasn't in the tomb, he ran directly to where He thought Jesus had been even though, as far as he knew, he was running straight into the danger of the Roman guards who had been assigned to it. Peter's repentance was made evident in his actions. His actions moved him toward Jesus. In fact, later, when Peter was fishing on his boat and Jesus showed up on the shore and called out to him, Peter jumped into the water to get to Jesus as fast as he could. His actions demonstrated a change of mind.

Be sure that what you call repentance is truly repentance and not simply remorse because you may have gotten caught, or are suffering the consequences of what you have done. Because only a repentance that reconnects you to a relationship with God leads to life, peace, and a cleansing of moral purity.

There is no greater example of Jesus' cleaning service toward a repentant sexual sinner than His encounter with the woman caught in adultery (John 8:1–11). If you're familiar with the story, you know that the whole scene came about because the Jews were always trying to set Jesus up with an unsolvable dilemma.

So they brought an immoral woman to Him, knowing that the Law declared that she should be stoned to death. They made it a point to explain to Jesus that she had been caught in the very act. "We caught her committing adultery. What do you say, Jesus?"

Since this was a public scene, we can imagine this

woman's sense of humiliation as she stood before the sin-less Son of God.

Instead of condemning her to death, Jesus responded to their accusation and demand by bending down and writing in the sand. Two thousand years' worth of Bible commentators have tried to figure out what Jesus wrote, but, whatever it was, He stood up and hit the scribes and Pharisees with something incredibly powerful when He said, "He who is without sin among you, let him be the first to throw a stone at her" (v. 7).

Then He started writing on the ground again as these self-righteous but equally guilty sinners melted away one by one into the crowd. When Jesus stood up the second time, no one was left but the woman and Him.

I think what Jesus wrote in the sand had to do with the correct reading of the law on adultery, because the scene before Him was messed up. The woman's accusers were only half right. If she was indeed caught in the act of adultery, this woman was deserving of the death penalty under the Mosaic law. But the law also stipulated that the man die as well.

However, these men did not bring the guilty man, even though they knew who this man was, since they caught them in "the very act." This showed that they weren't really interested in justice or God's honor or any of the things that mattered. If they were, there would have been two guilty people standing before Jesus, and not one. Instead, they were just using this woman by exploiting her shame to do their own dirty work of trapping Jesus.

So Jesus wrote once on the ground, and then twice. It is possible that He was saying that if we are going to condemn this woman by the law, then let's get the law straight. Two people have to die here, not one.

Then there was another thing. The stone thrower could not be guilty of the same crime as the accused. You could not pick up a stone and kill somebody else for committing adultery if you too had committed adultery, because then you would have to undergo the same sentence after they finished with the other person.

What I mean is that Jesus' statement about throwing the first stone is more specific than we usually understand it to be. This is usually interpreted to mean that Jesus was saying that a person had to be perfect before he could throw a stone at someone else.

But if that were the case, the law would never have been carried out even in the Old Testament economy, because there are no perfect people. Jesus is not talking about being perfect. He is saying that the only ones qualified to stone this woman were the ones who were not guilty of the same sin. That thinned the crowd out really quick. The men left one by one because Jesus could then condemn them to the same penalty of stoning if they were to cast a stone at the woman, since they had done the same thing themselves—perhaps with this same woman.

But the best part is what Jesus said to the woman. He saw into her heart and said, "I do not condemn you, either. Go. From now on sin no more" (John 8:11). That's the

word of forgiveness I leave with you if you have committed sexual sin.

You must bring it to Jesus with a repentant heart and
confess it. If you will do that, He will forgive you, and
you can go on your way restored, with His power avail-
able to keep you from falling into sexual sin again. Notice
that Jesus neither minimized this woman's sin nor pum-
meled her with it, as the others wanted to do. He recog-
nized it, forgave it, and told her to turn from it. What is
more, He did not condemn her because of it. Jesus specif-
ically said, "I do not condemn you, either. . . . From now
on sin no more." By removing her condemnation, He set
her free from shame and guilt—thus giving her the opportunity to go forward in her life without continuing in
sin.

So let me make a challenge to you today that if you
have lost your sexual purity, that you will reclaim it now.
Even if you are no longer a physical virgin, you can commit yourself to sexual purity and faithfulness from this
point forward. This is not to pretend that there is not
residual damage from sexual sin. Nor does it mean that
you are not experiencing any physical cravings or bond-
ing as a result of what you have done. You most likely are,
and because of that you need to be wise about how you
attempt to redirect your passions. But forgiveness means
you can stop the damage from continuing to occur now
and enjoy the blessing of purity from here on out.

If you are married, I urge you to renew your commitment to your partner. If you are still a virgin, make a vow

to God that you will remain pure until He brings some-body into your life through marriage. God will be a lot more responsive to your prayers about the future if you are living for Him now. Remember, true decisions are not made; they are lived. And keeping sex sacred is one of the most important decisions you could ever live out, both for now and for eternity.

Notes

Chapter 1: Sex as God Intended It

1. February 26, 2008. Copyright © 2008 by the American Academy of Pediatrics.
2. *Strong's Exhaustive Concordance*, #H3405.
3. Ibid., #G4203.
4. Ibid., #H7901.
5. Ibid., #G2853.
6. Arthur Aron and others, "Reward, Motivation, and Emotion Systems Associated with Early-Stage Intense Romantic Love," *Journal of Neurophysiology* 94 (2005): 327–337.

THE URBAN ALTERNATIVE

D r. Tony Evans and The Urban Alternative (TUA) equips, empowers, and unites Christians to impact individuals, families, churches, and communities to restore hope and transform lives.

We believe the core cause of the problems we face in our personal lives, homes, churches, and societies is a spiritual one; therefore, the only way to address them is spiritually. We've tried a political, a social, an economic, and even a religious agenda. It's time for a Kingdom Agenda—God's visible and comprehensive rule over every area of life because when we function as we were designed, there is a divine power that changes everything. It renews and restores as the life of Christ is made manifest within our own. As we align ourselves under Him, there is an alignment that happens from deep within—where He brings about full restoration. It is an atmosphere that revives and makes whole.

As it impacts us, it impacts others—transforming every sphere of life in which we live. When each biblical sphere of life functions in accordance with God's Word, the outcomes are evangelism, discipleship, and community impact. As we learn how to govern ourselves under God, we then transform the institutions of family, church, and society from a biblically based kingdom perspective. Where, through Him, we are touching heaven and changing earth.

To achieve our goal we use a variety of strategies, methods, and resources for reaching and equipping as many people as possible.

BROADCAST MEDIA

Hundreds of thousands of individuals experience *The Alternative with Dr. Tony Evans* through the daily radio broadcast playing on nearly **1,000 radio outlets** and in over **130 countries**. The broadcast can also be seen on several television networks, and is viewable online at TonyEvans.org.

LEADERSHIP TRAINING

The Kingdom Agenda Pastors (KAP) provides a *viable network* for *like-minded pastors* who embrace the Kingdom

Agenda philosophy. Pastors have the opportunity to go deeper with Dr. Tony Evans as they are given greater biblical knowledge, practical applications, and resources to impact individuals, families, churches, and communities. KAP welcomes *senior and associate pastors* of all churches.

The Kingdom Agenda Pastors' Summit progressively develops church leaders to meet the demands of the 21st century while maintaining the gospel message and the strategic position of the church. The Summit introduces *intensive seminars, workshops,* and *resources,* addressing issues affecting the community, family, leadership, organizational health and more.

Pastors' Wives Ministry, founded by Dr. Lois Evans, provides *counsel, encouragement,* and *spiritual resources* for pastors' wives as they serve with their husbands in the ministry. A primary focus of the ministry is the KAP Summit that offers senior pastors' wives a safe place to *reflect, renew,* and *relax* along with training in personal development, spiritual growth, and care for their emotional and physical well-being.

COMMUNITY IMPACT

National Church Adopt-A-School Initiative (NCAASI) prepares churches across the country to impact communities by using *public schools as the primary vehicle for effecting positive social change* in urban youth and families. Leaders of churches, school districts, faith-based organizations, and other nonprofit organizations are equipped with the knowledge and tools to *forge partnerships* and *build strong social service delivery systems*. This training is based on the comprehensive church-based community impact strategy conducted by Oak Cliff Bible Fellowship. It addresses such areas as economic development, education, housing, health revitalization, family renewal, and racial reconciliation. We also assist churches in tailoring the model to meet the specific needs of their communities while simultaneously addressing the spiritual and moral frame of reference.

RESOURCE DEVELOPMENT

We are fostering lifelong learning partnerships with the people we serve by providing a variety of published materials. We offer booklets, Bible studies, books, CDs, and DVDs to strengthen people in their walk with God and ministry to others.

* * *

For more information, a catalog of Dr. Tony Evans'
ministry resources, and a complimentary copy of
Dr. Evans' devotional newsletter,
call (800) 800-3222
or write to TUA at P.O. Box 4000, Dallas TX 75208,
or log on to
www.TonyEvans.org

EVANS
THE URBAN ALTERNATIVE

At The Urban Alternative, the national ministry of Dr. Tony Evans, we seek to restore hope and transform lives to reflect the values of the kingdom of God. Along with our community outreach initiative, leadership training and family and personal growth emphasis, Dr. Evans continues to minister to people from the pulpit to the heart as the relevant expositor with the powerful voice. Lives are touched both locally and abroad through our daily radio broadcast, weekly television ministry and internet access points.

Presenting an
ALTERNATIVE to:

Community Outreach

Equipping leaders to engage public schools and communities with mentoring, family support services and a commitment to a brighter tomorrow.

Leadership Training

Offering an exclusive opportunity for pastors and their wives to receive discipleship from Drs. Tony and Lois Evans and the TUA staff, along with networking opportunities, resources and encouragement.

Family and Personal Growth

Strengthening homes and deepening spiritual lives through helpful resources that encourage hope and health for the glory of God.

TonyEvans.org

MOODYRADIO

Where you turn. For life.

Moody Radio produces and delivers compelling programs filled with biblical insights and creative expressions of faith that help you take the next step in your relationship with Christ.

You can hear Moody Radio on 36 stations and more than 1,500 radio outlets across the U.S. and Canada. Or listen on your smartphone with the Moody Radio app!

www.moodyradio.org

urbanpraise

Urban Praise, a commercial-free Moody Radio Internet station, offers a soulful blend of rich gospel and urban music. Energize your faith with artists like Kirk Franklin, Israel Houghton, Shirley Caesar, CeCe Winans, Walter Hawkins, and Lecrae, along with bite-size teaching segments from Tony Evans, Crawford Loritts, Melvin Banks, Beth Moore, and others.

www.urbanpraiseradio.org

MOODYRADIO

Where you turn. For life.